SAILING PAST THE POINT

by

Bernard McCall

In 1989 Erwin Strahlmann bought a part share in a ship. By 2004 he owned a fleet of over fifty coastal vessels, most of which had been bought on the second-hand market. He had also placed an order for new ships. This order had been given to the Slovenské Lodenice shipyard at Komárno on the River Danube in Slovakia and was for eleven vessels of the "Rhein" design. This shipyard had opened in 1898 and had concentrated on building and repairing inland vessels for use on the Danube but from the 1960s it had built large numbers of sea/river ships for Russia. The Rhein design was very successful during the 1990s but towards the end of that decade the yard was cut off from the sea after NATO forces had bombed bridges over the Danube in Serbia, downstream from Komárno, thus cutting off its link to the sea. Having been declared bankrupt in 2001, the yard then re-opened and was able to resume production after the repair of the bridges. The *Suderau* (ATG, 2461gt/05) was launched on 2 May 2005 and delivered on 3 July. We see her on passage from Bromborough to Sharpness to load scrap for Santander on 24 April 2011.

Hopefully this image gives something of the atmosphere of Battery Point. Out of sight to the right is an outdoor swimming pool and popular cafe. There is an alternative view on page 35.

INTRODUCTION

Without doubt Battery Point in Portishead is one of the best locations in the UK to watch ships as they pass by. Shipping enthusiasts will stake the claims of other viewing points such as Calshot but it is difficult to surpass the variety of ships seen at Battery Point – and their closeness to the observer on land. To illustrate this variety, we published *Passing the Point* in 2005 and *Still Passing the Point* in 2010. Like everything else shipping is subject to change and variation. The changes in the Bristol Channel shipping scene over the last twelve years have been considerable. The most significant one is the virtual ending of coal imports which used to arrive in bulk carriers for onward transmission to power stations. In 2013 the British government introduced the Carbon Price Floor tax to dissuade power generators from using coal. This resulted in the premature closure of some power stations and a huge reduction in coal imports.

With the loss of income from the bulk carriers, the Bristol Port Company sought other sources of revenue and one of these was passenger shipping. Although cruise ships had called occasionally, the company had never been keen on this shipping sector but from 2013 it actively encouraged visits by cruise vessels. It has been able to overcome problems posed by security and health & safety issues. Another trade to have virtually disappeared is the import of refrigerated produce. We are aware of only one refrigerated vessel to have called during the last five years.

Many enthusiasts have been pleased to see the re-appearance of container ships from the fleet of the Mediterranean Shipping Company (MSC). This company's ships often have an interesting history and a selection appeared in previous books.

In 2011, a change in policy saw smaller, more modern (and less interesting) ships appear, often on short term charters. However, MSC's triangular service linking Royal Portbury Dock to Antwerp and Dunkirk, changed to one linking Antwerp to a French port (usually Le Havre and/or Brest) and Liverpool in addition to Royal Portbury Dock. This required bigger ships handling more containers and so ships from the MSC fleet are calling once again.

Inevitably there have been changes in towage too. The need for a relatively large tug fleet diminished once the bulk carriers ceased to call. On busy tides it was always possible to summon extra tugs from the Cory / Svitzer fleet in South Wales. That is no longer possible as towage in South Wales is now handled by a different company rather than Svitzer. As is explained within this book, extra tugs must now come from Swansea or even Milford Haven.

The photographs have been arranged in small groups to illustrate the various types of ships which pass Battery Point. There are now various websites which purport to feature the passing shipping. In fact most of these offer little information other than basic (and sometimes incorrect) details cribbed from other websites. I hope that this book will provide interesting details about the ships, their builders, their cargoes, and, where appropriate, their significance within the wider maritime world.

My grateful thanks go to Chris Jones, of the The Bristol Port Company, for his invaluable assistance; to John Vickers (Safe Fix) for pre-press work; to Gil Mayes, for checking early drafts, and to Gomer Press, for the finished product.

Bernard McCall,   Portishead,   April 2017

Published by Bernard McCall, 400 Nore Road, Portishead, Bristol, BS20 8EZ, England. Website : www.coastalshipping.co.uk
Telephone/fax : 01275 846178. Email : bernard@coastalshipping.co.uk. All distribution enquiries should be addressed to the publisher.

Printed by Gomer Press, Llandysul Enterprise Park, Llandysul, Ceredigion, Wales, SA44 4JL.
Telephone : 01559 36237   Fax : 01559 363758   Email : sales@gomer.co.uk   Website : www.gomerprinting.co.uk

Front cover : The number of coastal ship owners based in the UK has continued to fall since we published *Still Passing the Point*. There is one company, however, which has gone against the trend and has expanded; this company is Faversham Ships which, as its name implies, was once based in Kent but which now has its headquarters at Cowes on the Isle of Wight. The *Islay Trader* (BRB, 1512gt/92) is one of four sisterships acquired from a German owner. The first of five sisterships, she was launched at the Rosslauer shipyard on the River Elbe on 7 November 1991 and was completed as *Lass Moon* for Hamburg-based owner H H Wübbe. She was renamed *Islay Trader* in 2007 when she entered the Faversham fleet along with three of her sisterships. We see her inward bound on 15 August 2016 with a cargo of fertiliser from Sluiskil. She often visits the Scottish island after which she is named as she delivers malting barley to the Islay distilleries.

Back cover : The vast majority of enthusiasts like to take their photographs with an uncluttered background as offered from the headland. Whilst the majority of the photographs in these albums have followed this principle, we hope that we have been able to suggest alternative viewpoints. As a final example we see the *Svitzer Bevois* (GBR, 250gt/85), launched at the McTay Marine shipyard, Bromborough, on 2 June 1985 and completed on 22 August. She was built for service in the Solent for the Southampton Isle of Wight and South of England Royal Mail Steam Packet Company Limited, better known as Red Funnel. Originally named *Sir Bevois*, the legendary founder of Southampton, she became *Svitzer Bevois* in 2007. The photograph is dated 14 June 2013. On 1 December 2014 she was renamed *Beaver* following sale to Swedish owners and twelve days later she departed for the Swedish port of Gävle. Her name was soon amended to *Tug Beaver*.

Whenever a cruise ship sails by, there is always a large gathering of people on Battery Point. Some are enthusiasts, others are friends and relatives of passengers on the ship. The arrival or departure of the *Marco Polo* (BHS, 22080gt/65) is always especially popular, partly because of her long and fascinating history. She was launched on 25 April 1964 at the Mathias-Thesen shipyard in Warnemunde and completed on 14 August 1965 as *Aleksandr Pushkin* for the Russian state-controlled merchant fleet. She was built to serve a transatlantic route linking Leningrad (St Petersburg) to Montreal. Her career during the Soviet era is not generally agreed. She was laid up in Singapore in 1990 and was later sent to Greece for a major overhaul and upgrade which lasted over two years. During this time, she was renamed *Marco Polo*. It was in 2010 that she was taken over by Cruise & Maritime Voyages, a newly-established company based in the UK. The next page gives more information about Cruise & Maritime Voyages. We see *Marco Polo* arriving back from a cruise to the West Indies on 31 March 2016 prior to embarking passengers for a cruise to Norway.

With the Bristol Port Company seeking to market the port for cruise passengers, an Essex-based company called Cruise & Maritime Voyages came in to fulfil the requirement. The company had been formed as recently as 2009 and sought to offer no-fly cruising from British ports using ships of small and medium size with an intimate atmosphere. This arrangement was ideal for Bristol and for the cruise company. The start was inauspicious. Passengers for the first cruise on **Discovery** (BMU, 20216gt/71) had to be taken by coach to Portland because of a delay in her refit. At Portland the ship was detained by the Maritime and Coastguard Agency and her passengers had to be brought back. Later released from detention, she

was able to leave Avonmouth for the next cruise on 15 March and here we see her outward bound to Dublin in fading light on 7 April 2013. She was launched as **Island Princess** at the Rheinstahl Nordseewerke shipyard in Emden on 6 March 1971 and delivered as **Island Discovery** on 4 January 1972. She featured in a television series called *The Love Boat* which is claimed to have revolutionised the cruise industry. After a short-lived career as a pilgrim ship in Korea, she was sold and renamed **Platinum**, becoming **Discovery** in 2002. The year 2014 proved to be her last. After suffering mechanical problems she was sold for recycling and was beached at Alang in December 2014.

The **Azores** (PMD, 16488gt/48), inward bound on 17 May 2015 from St Mary's, Scilly Isles, after a round-Britain cruise, has a long history packed with incidents. She was launched at the Gotaverken shipyard in Gothenburg on 9 September 1946 and completed for the Swedish America Line as **Stockholm** in February 1948. Although the largest passenger ship built in Sweden at the time, she was the smallest passenger ship then operating a liner service on the North Atlantic. On the night of 25 July 1956, she collided with the Italian liner **Andrea Doria** in heavy fog off Nantucket. A total of 51 people lost their lives and the collision gained notoriety as it involved two passenger vessels. The ship was sold in 1960 to the government of the German Democratic Republic (East Germany) and was renamed **Volkerfreundschaft**. For 25 years, she provided cruises for the Freien Deutschen Gewerkschaftsbundes (FDGB) (Free German Trade Union Federation). She was sold and renamed **Volker** in 1985, being laid up for a while in Southampton before becoming an accommodation vessel for asylum seekers in Oslo under the name **Fridtjof Nansen**. She was then extensively refurbished in Italy and renamed firstly **Italia 1** and in 1994 **Italia Prima**.

We now continue the history of the **Azores**. As **Italia Prima**, she was sold and renamed **Valtur Prima**, working mainly in the Caribbean with Cuba as a popular destination. Indeed there were many Cubans working as crew at that time. After a period laid up in Cuba in 2001, she was sold to Festival Cruise Lines and renamed **Caribe** in 2002. Three years later she became **Athena** for Classic International Cruises. There were reports that she fended off an attack by pirates in the Gulf of Aden in December 2008 but some of these reports seem to have been exaggerated. Early in 2013 she was bought by Portuscale Cruises after being detained because her previous owners had failed to pay bills. Renamed **Azores**, she was chartered in 2015 by Cruise & Maritime Voyages and was renamed **Astoria** for the 2016 season. On 9 May 2016 the **Astoria** was inward bound from Eidfjord at the end of a cruise to the Norwegian fjords. She sailed to Honfleur on the next tide.

The sleek lines of the **Funchal** (PMD, 9563gt/61) are evident as she passes Battery Point on the afternoon of 6 October 2014 at the start of a voyage to Stavanger and the Norwegian fjords. She was launched by Helsingør Værft in Denmark on 10 February 1961 and delivered in October of that year. Although she served as the yacht of the Portuguese president for a time, she had a chequered career with perhaps the most successful time being a period from 1984 when she served the British cruise market. The bankruptcy of her owners in 2012 led to fears that she would be broken up but she was bought by a Portuguese entrepreneur in early 2013 and given a complete refit during which her traditional white hull was repainted black. She was taken over by Cruise & Maritime Voyages to replace the **Discovery** which had been sold for recycling.

The **Europa** (BHS, 28890gt/99) was launched at the Helsinki shipyard of Kvaerner Masa on 4 March 1999 and completed on 9 September. Refurbished in 2007, she is owned by Hapag-Lloyd, a well-known German shipping company, and they are keen to proclaim that the ship takes a maximum of 400 passengers which is a mere 10% of the number taken by some modern cruise vessels. She has a crew of 285 and has been consistently voted to be the best cruise ship currently in service. She called at Avonmouth on 16 May 2016 as part of a cruise from Hamburg to France, the UK and Ireland. She had not ordered tugs to assist her departure and, as a consequence, she found herself pinned against the eastern breakwater by a strong westerly wind and had to wait two hours until a tug could be summoned. It was almost 7.00pm when she passed Battery Point on passage to Milford Haven.

The **Maersk Windhoek** (PAN, 17280gt/09), inward bound from Antwerp on 30 October 2013, was launched at the Imabari Zosen shipyard in Japan on 23 February 2009 and completed for Japanese owners on 17 April. Shipbuilding at Imabari started in 1901 and the Imabari Shipbuilding Co Ltd began in 1942 following the consolidation of several yards. The first steel ship was built in 1956. It has now become one of the main shipbuilders in Japan with nine shipyards and three business centres; over ninety ships are built each year. On charter from new to Maersk Lines, the **Maersk Windhoek** was sublet to the Mediterranean Shipping Company for its Antwerp – Dunkirk – Bristol service from mid-February until early November 2013. She was renamed **Windhoek** in March 2016. On 20 September she was attacked by pirates when at anchor off Conakry. Her crew were used as hostages whilst the pirates ransacked the crew's cabins and other areas of the ship. Thankfully there were no injuries and the crew were released as the pirates made their getaway.

The **MSC Ishyka** (LBR, 25713gt/97) was launched at the Daewoo shipyard in Okpo, South Korea, on 13 September 1997 and she was completed on 5 December. She is typical of many handy-sized container ships built in the late 1990s that were hugely popular with charterers. Her history of name changes reflects this popularity. Owned in Germany she was launched as **Conti Cartagena** but entered service on charter to Sea-Land as **Sea-Land Argentina**. In December 2000 she began a one-year charter to the Mediterranean Shipping Company as **MSC Provence** and reverted to **Conti Cartagena** in December 2001. Later charters saw her become **CMA CGM Eagle** (2003-2004), **Cap Pilar** (2005-2007), **MOL Splendour** (2007-2009), and then **MSC Ishyka** from April 2014. She was photographed on 12 March 2016.

The **MSC Namibia II** (LBR, 23953gt/91) was launched at the Hyundai shipyard in Ulsan, South Korea, on 29 June 1991 and completed as **CMB Drive** on 20 August. She made only two voyages under this name, being delivered as such from Ulsan to Keelung and from there to Hong Kong where she was renamed **China Sea**. A new charter saw her become **Ibn Khaldoun** in mid-March 1994 when she commenced trade linking Middle Eastern ports such as Jeddah and Dubai to Hong Kong and Singapore. The service was later extended to include European ports such as Valencia, Antwerp and Felixstowe. By 1997, she was trading mainly in the Mediterranean and on 20 November she switched to the American flag as **Endeavor**. She remained in the Mediterranean but there were occasional transatlantic voyages to New York. In March 2006 she was chartered by Maersk and was renamed **Maersk Vermont**. Her charter to the Mediterranean Shipping Company began in March 2011 and it will be seen that she retained her owner's funnel colours rather than those of MSC as she passed Battery Point on a rather dull 6 March 2016.

The **MSC Santhya** (PAN, 37071gt/91), outward bound to Brest on 12 April 2016, was built at the Bremer Vulkan shipyard at Vegesack, Bremen. She was launched on 3 February 1991 and completed as **Vladivostok** during May. She had the distinction of being the first of ten ships built at the yard for Sovcomflot, the Russian state shipping company. Only a few months after her delivery, the communist regime in Russia collapsed and the ship was taken over by DSR-Senator Lines and renamed **DSR Senator**.

DSR was the abbreviation for Deutsche Seereederei, the former state-operated merchant fleet of the German Democratic Republic (East Germany). This had been privatised and merged with the fleet of Senator Linie, dating from 1985. She became **Baykal Senator** in 2000 and **MSC Santhya** in 2004 after purchase by the Mediterranean Shipping Company. Between 2012 and 2014 she traded between ports in the southern United States and South America.

Inward bound in fast-fading light on 2 December 2014, the *MSC Eyra* (PAN, 21586gt/82) is one of the older and more interesting MSC container ships to have appeared. She was built at the Warnowwerft shipyard in Warnemunde, near Rostock, and was completed as *Kapitan Kozlovskiy* in late November 1982. She was the third of ten examples of a design known as Mercur II. At the time they were the largest container ships in the Russian merchant fleet and, like her sisterships, she was lengthened by 30 metres in 1989. Between 20 April and 19 October 1995 she was chartered by Compagnie Generale Maritime for a series of voyages from Hamburg and Bremerhaven to ports in South Africa; for this she was renamed *CGM Le Cap*. On completion of the charter she was renamed *Miden Agan* and became *Maersk Toronto* in 1997. She reverted to *Miden Agan* in 2000 and then *Pelineo* on 23 November 2002 before being bought by the Mediterranean Shipping Company and renamed *MSC Eyra* at Piraeus on 14 February 2004.

The **MSC America** (PAN, 34231gt/93) made a handful of calls in mid-2015 and we see her inward bound from Antwerp on 24 July. She was another vessel that had begun life with DSR-Senator Lines which had emerged from the former state-controlled East German merchant fleet. She was launched at the Thyssen Nordseewerke yard in Emden on 18 September 1992 and delivered as **DSR America** on 5 February 1993. She was the penultimate example of a group of six container ships identified as the BV-2700 type, two of which came from the Emden yard. She was sold and renamed **America Senator** in 2000 and then **MSC America** when taken on charter by MSC in 2004. As a general rule, ships chartered by MSC have a geographical name whilst owned ships use a girl's name.

Whilst the container ships of the Mediterranean Shipping Company have become a common sight in the Bristol Channel since the 1990s, it is much more unusual to see one of the company's vehicle carriers. The **MSC Cristiana** (PAN, 59835gt/11) was a very rare caller indeed and we see her outward bound to Tilbury on 5 May 2014. Whilst most large vehicle carriers are built in Japan or South Korea, the **MSC Cristiana** was built by STX Dalian at Wafangdian in China along with a sistership, **MSC Immacolata**. She was completed in December 2011. STX is in fact a South Korean company and was once the fourth largest shipbuilder in the world. The Dalian yard began to suffer financial problems in June 2014 and was declared bankrupt in March 2015 following the failure of a restructuring programme.

The initials NOCC stand for Norwegian Car Carriers, a company formed in 2010 through the amalgamation of Eidsiva Rederi ASA (founded in 1930) and Dyvi Shipping AS (founded in 1955). Both companies had extensive ro/ro and car carrier experience with Dyvi Shipping AS having taken delivery of **Dyvi Anglia**, the world's first purpose-built roll-on roll-off car carrier, in 1964. The **NOCC Caribbean** (SGP, 42447gt/88) passes Battery Point on 27 May 2012 at the end of a voyage from the Far East. She was built by Hyundai at Ulsan, being launched on 4 January 1988 and completed as **Cypress Pass** on 8 March. She became **NOCC Caribbean** in early 2011 and then was renamed **Silver Soul** in November 2012. The commemorative stone in the foreground was set up by the North Somerset Branch of the Merchant Navy Association in 2005 and is dedicated to all West Country seafarers who have passed the Point in times of peace and war since the Middle Ages, some of whom never returned.

The **Michigan Highway** (JPN, 56951gt/08) was launched by Shin Kurushima Toyohashi Shipbuilding on 28 November 2007 and completed on 15 February 2008. This shipbuilding company was established in May 1987. The ship is owned by Kawasaki Kisen Kaisha Ltd, better known as K-Line and established in 1919. It is one of the leading shipping companies in Japan and owns ships of every kind in addition to vehicle carriers. This vessel is named after a road in the USA which has gained notoriety for the number of multi-vehicle crashes it has witnessed. We see her outward bound to Halifax in Canada on the afternoon of 15 August 2016 having arrived from Bremerhaven and Southampton on the previous day.

The **Porgy** (PAN, 58752gt/09) made a comparatively rare visit to northern Europe in early October 2014. She arrived at Royal Portbury Dock on 5 October and we see her leaving the following day. She was on her way to Bremerhaven and called at Zeebrugge before heading to Port Elizabeth. She was launched at the Toyohashi Shipbuilding yard on 24 March 2009 and completed on 8 June. Wallenius Wilhelmsen Logistics was established in 1999 and is owned on a 50/50 basis by Wallenius Lines, based in Sweden, and Wilh. Wilhelmsen ASA, based in Norway. The ships from each company retain that company's colours and naming scheme so the **Porgy** wears traditional Wallenius colours and follows that company's naming scheme using the titles of operas. (Yes – she does have a sistership named **Bess**.) The joint company operates over fifty vessels on 12 trade routes.

The **Autosun** arrives each week with Vauxhall cars made at the General Motors factory in Zaragosa and exported from the Spanish port of Pasajes. She is often assisted by another vessel from the UECC fleet and on 8 February 2013 the **Autopride** (PMD, 11591gt/77) called. Surprisingly she is rarely seen in the Bristol Channel and usually trades from Pasajes to Bremerhaven with additional calls at other ports such as Southampton and/or Zeebrugge. Rather unusually for a vehicle carrier, she was built at a shipyard in northern Europe, namely the Frisian Welgelegen yard in Harlingen. She was launched on 17 June 1997 and completed on 16 October.

The **Auto Eco** (PMD, 42424gt/16) was built by Kawasaki Heavy Industries at its Nantong Cosco shipyard in China and delivered on 29 September 2016. She was officially named at Zeebrugge on 21 November but prior to that she called at Royal Portbury Dock on 9 November with Mitsubishi L200 vehicles on her maiden voyage from Japan. She is owned by United European Car Carriers (UECC), a partnership between Japanese shipowner Nippon Yusen Kaisa (NYK) and Swedish company Wallenius Lines. Classed as a pure car and truck carrier (PCTC), she is a unique vessel in being the only example of her type to be dual-fuel LNG powered using both heavy oil and LNG; she is able to make a 14-day voyage around the world solely on LNG and without needing to be refuelled. Furthermore, she has been built to the highest possible ice class which enables her to trade into the Baltic and far north of Russia. She can carry 3800 cars and will be followed by a sister vessel, **Auto Energy**.

Having arrived from the River Tyne on the previous day, the **Hoegh Kunsan** (SGP, 44219gt/96) had just started a voyage to Tangier when photographed on 6 February 2013. She was built in Japan with her hull being constructed by Hashihama Zosen at Tadotsu and completed at the Tsuneishi shipyard in Numakuma on 1 March 1996. She was one of four sister vessels built for A P Møller-Maersk and entered service as **Maersk Taiyo**. Leif Höegh & Co was established in 1927 and became well-known for its ownership of oil tankers and later ore/bulk/oil carriers. In 1970 it joined with Ugland to form Höegh Ugland Auto Liners (HUAL) and in 2000 bought out the other 50% of HUAL. The company was renamed Höegh Autoliners in 2005. Three years later, Höegh Autoliners took over a fleet of twelve car carriers from A P Møller-Maersk and the **Maersk Taiyo** became **Hoegh Kunsan**. As part of the deal, A P Møller-Maersk became a minority shareholder with 37.5% of the shares in Höegh Autoliners.

The *City of Mumbai* (SGP, 27887gt/87) was launched by the Mitsui Engineering & Shipbuilding Co Ltd at Tamano in Japan on 12 March 1987 and completed as *Maersk Sun* on 24 July. As we note on page 20, Höegh took over the Maersk fleet of vehicle carriers and she was renamed *Hoegh Mumbai* at Yokohama on 9 April 2008, becoming *City of Mumbai* on 1 September in the same year. She was one of several vehicle carriers used to transport Nissan cars from the River Tyne, a trade that began in 1996 and ten years after the Nissan factory opened at nearby Washington. The *City of Mumbai* arrived from the River Tyne on the evening of 27 May 2012 and we see her leaving on her way to Tangiers on the following morning. She left northern Europe in January 2013 and now trades exclusively in the Far East.

The Airbus A380 aircraft is constructed from parts made on several sites. The centre and aft parts of the fuselage are built in Hamburg, the wings in Mostyn, the tail in Cadiz and the nose in Saint Nazaire. This aircraft was followed by the A400M, a turboprop military aircraft whose wings are manufactured at Filton, on the outskirts of Bristol, with eventual construction at Seville. The design of a vessel to transport the large aircraft sections was entrusted to French shipowners Louis Dreyfus Armateurs (LDA). The

City of Hamburg (RIF, 15643gt/08) was constructed as a collaborative project between LDA and Leif Höegh. She wears the funnel colours of both companies. She was launched on 23 February 2008 at the yard of Singapore Technologies Marine, officially named on 11 June and delivered on 4 December. She was followed by a sistership and both were chartered to Airbus for twenty years. We see her passing Battery Point on 28 June 2013 at the start of a voyage to Mostyn with a cargo of aircraft wings.

Seatruck Ferries was established in 1996 and is the only UK-based freight-only ferry company operating on the Irish Sea. Its ferries have traditionally traded from Liverpool and Heysham to Dublin and Warrenpoint. However a casual conversation with a lorry driver about delivering Honda cars by road from Bristol to the north-west of England for export to Ireland caused the company to consider a weekly service from Royal Portbury Dock. The *Seatruck Pace* (CYP, 14759gt/09) is seen outward bound to Dublin on the first sailing on 16 October 2016 and subsequent sailings have always been on a Sunday. The third of four sisterships, she was built by Astilleros de Huelva and was launched as *Clipper Pace* on 22 December 2007. She entered service on the Liverpool – Dublin route in March 2009. She was renamed *Seatruck Pace* in February 2012 and in May of that year she was chartered to DFDS for its service linking Rosyth to Zeebrugge, making her first sailing from Rosyth on 15 May. She returned to Heysham to resume Irish Sea crossings on 7 July 2012. She has three decks and can accommodate 120 trailers.

The **Grande Scandinavia** (ITA, 52485gt/01), inward bound on 16 May 2012, is one of five ships operating Grimaldi's Euromed service. After leaving Royal Portbury, the usual rotation sees visits to Cork, Esbjerg, Wallhamn, Antwerp and Southampton before heading to Salerno, Piraeus, Izmir, Alexandria, Limassol and Ashdod. She was launched at the Daewoo shipyard in Okpo, South Korea, on 16 December 2000 and was delivered to Grimaldi on 27 March 2001. Grimaldi has earned a reputation for the efficient transport of railway vehicles. It has shipped the trains for the Rome metro from Spain to Italy and those for the Madrid metro from Italy to Spain. It was also involved in the shipment of trains for the Jerusalem metro. In October 2009, the **Grande Scandinavia** transported from Antwerp to Izmir two underground carriage prototypes built by Alstom of France for the Istanbul metro.

The **Grande Benin** (ITA, 47120gt/09) was launched at the Uljanik shipyard in Pula, Croatia, on 25 April 2009 and completed on 27 August. The yard was founded in 1856 as the shipyard of the Austro-Hungarian navy. In autumn 2015, she was one of six Grimaldi ships offering passenger accommodation on a new service linking Civitavecchia (near Rome) to Baltimore, Ohio. It was expected that other ports in North America would soon be added. As her name would suggest, she usually works on Grimaldi's West African service which sails out of Tilbury but on 9 November 2016 she arrived at Royal Portbury Dock when working on the Euro – Aegean service of Grimaldi Lines which links ports in the Mediterranean to ports in the UK and northern Europe.

Founded in 1947, the Grimaldi shipping empire is huge and includes companies trading in Finland, Greece, Malta, transatlantic trades and, of course, its traditional base in the Mediterranean. We tend to see a limited number of its vessels that operate a liner service linking northern Europe to the Mediterranean. The usual trading pattern of the *Eurocargo Cagliari* (ITA, 32647gt/12) sees her delivering cars from Valencia to Livorno and Savona but on 18 April 2013 she visited Royal Portbury Dock with a special delivery of Fiat, Citroen and Peugeot vehicles from Salerno. She sailed on to Antwerp before returning to Valencia. She was built at the Hyundai Mipo shipyard in Ulsan, South Korea, and delivered in May 2012. She was involved in a sad incident in late November 2015 when a stevedore was crushed between two "mafis" (cargo trailers) during loading at Valencia.

The **Strait of Magellan** (GBR, 29429gt/11) was built by Odense Staalskibsværft at Lindø, near Odense. She was launched on 18 March 2011 and completed on 25 August. She sailed direct to lay-up at Tilbury, arriving on 30 August, and later moved to Avonmouth where she arrived on 15 June 2012. We see her at the start of a passage to Falmouth on 2 October 2012. Sistership **Bering Strait** was also laid up at Avonmouth and she departed for Falmouth one week later. They were two of six ships ordered by Pacific Basin Shipping but this company decided to abandon roll on / roll off shipping and all six were eventually sold to Grimaldi with delivery through to 2015 and the new owner taking the ships on charter until completion of purchase. At Falmouth both ships underwent refurbishment for their new role. The **Strait of Magellan** was renamed **Eurocargo Catania** and as such left Falmouth on 2 November 2012 heading for the Mediterranean where she joined Grimaldi's network of routes.

Although some ships are seen fairly often, and there are regular trades to and from our local ports, surprises do happen. A good example was the arrival from Amsterdam of the **Birka Trader** (FIN, 12433gt/98) on 26 June 2013. We see her outward bound on the next day, giving Algeçiras as her destination. That may have been a stop for refuelling. In fact she was taking a cargo of second-hand cars to Libya. After arrival in the Mediterranean she was renamed **Trader** and became **Finnmaster** in early 2016. She was launched at Galati in Romania on 17 December 1997 with completion at the Fosen yard in Rissa, Norway, in May 1998. Originally named **United Trader**, she became **Birka Trader** in 2002.

Work on lock gates at Liverpool in mid-May 2012 meant that some vessels had to be diverted at very short notice. One of the companies affected was Atlantic Container Line (ACL) and its **Atlantic Conveyor** (SWE, 58438gt/85) was diverted to Royal Portbury Dock on her regular transatlantic crossing from Halifax, Nova Scotia. This came as little surprise as ACL is part of the Grimaldi group. With a length of 292 metres, she gained the distinction of becoming the longest ship ever to visit the port when she berthed on 15 May 2012.

Despite strong squalls, she docked easily with the assistance of three tugs and departed on the next tide. Built at the Swan Hunter shipyard at Wallsend and launched on 12 July 1984, she was lengthened by 42 metres in 1987. Readers may recall that the previous **Atlantic Conveyor** had been sunk during the Falklands campaign in late May 1982 with the tragic loss of eight of her crew including her master.

The visit by the **Atlantic Conveyor** on 15 May 2012 had a knock-on effect. From Liverpool, some containers brought by Atlantic Container Line ships require onward delivery to Ireland using feeder ships of Coastal Container Line. Consequently on 16 May 2012, the **Coastal Isle** (ATG, 3125gt/91) called to collect containers for delivery to Dublin. She was launched on 9 October 1991 at the Krögerwerft shipyard at Schacht-Audorf situated just east of Rendsburg in the Kiel Canal and was completed as **Johanna** on 26 November. She became **Coastal Isle** on 22 September 1997. Sold in 2013, she was renamed **Arslan II** and in the following year left northern Europe to become **Nargys H** and then **Captain Omar** under the flag of Togo. She left Dublin for Aliaga in Turkey on 25 March 2014 and in late 2016 was trading mainly between ports in Egypt.

In Marseille in 1978, Jacques Saade founded Compagnie Maritime d'Affrètement (CMA). It had four employees, one ship and one route (Marseille – Beirut – Lattakia – Livorno). In 1996, Compagnie Générale Maritime (CGM) was privatised by the French government and retained only its cargo services. After a three-year struggle it merged with CMA and the combined CMA CGM soon became hugely successful. On two or three occasions the company had tried to establish a feeder service to Bristol and other west coast ports but without success. In 2013, however, it was able to find the right balance of ports to be served and it has become successful.

The **AHS St. Georg** (MHL, 10384gt/98), outward bound to Liverpool on 28 May 2013, is one of the company's chartered ships to be used. She was launched on 20 May 1997 at the Sedef Gemi Endustrisi shipyard in Tuzla, Turkey, and delivered to Turkish owners as **Besiree Kalkavan** on 5 January 1998. Once in service she traded mainly from Turkish ports to Genoa, Barcelona and Marseilles but also included visits to New York. In 2006 she was sold to German owner Carsten Rehder and was renamed **Clou Ocean**, becoming **Veno di Nortada** for the duration of a charter between 2009 and 2011. She was renamed **AHS St Georg** in 2013.

The **Wes Monica** (ATG, 5629gt/09) was launched at the Jiangsu Yangzijiang shipyard (Jiangsu New Yangzi Shipbuilding Co Ltd) on 28 December 2008 and completed as **Monica C** on 31 March 2009. The shipyard in Jingjiang city was founded on 12 May 2005 and builds mainly large and medium-sized ships. It has the capacity to build 30 vessels or 3 million deadweight tonnes each year. This vessel was renamed **Wes Monica** in March 2014. On 19 December that year she was asked by the Greek Maritime Rescue Co-ordination Centre to go to the assistance of a fishing boat with 196 Syrian refugees on board. This boat had sprung a leak when on passage from Turkey to Italy. The master of the **Wes Monica** took responsibility for the situation and prepared to rescue the refugees if necessary. With help from three other ships he was able to monitor the situation until the arrival of two Italian coastguard vessels. We see her arriving on 15 February 2016 with fertiliser from Arzew in Algeria; she sailed to Hamburg four days later.

Huelin-Renouf had been involved in trade between the Channel Islands and the mainland for over eighty years when it was suddenly placed in liquidation in August 2013. It had taken the *Huelin Endeavour* (IRL, 2046gt/83) on charter in 2009. She was the second of the pair of Type 105a container feeder ships from the J J Sietas shipyard and was launched as *Neptunus* on 18 April 1983. She underwent trials on 10 May and on the following day was delivered to John Luhrs, of Wischhafen, as *Craigantlet* to trade between Garston and Belfast. The "Craig" prefix was a traditional one used by vessels of Hugh Craig & Co, coal and general merchants in Belfast. On 27 June 1988 she reverted to *Neptunus*, becoming *Pellworm* in 1995 and then

Coastal Wave in 1998 when taken on charter by Coastal Container Line. It was in August 2009 that she became *Huelin Endeavour*. She spent four months service on the Cardiff – Warrenpoint service of Coastal Container Line. On completion of her time on this service, she arrived on 15 April 2012 and we see her outward bound to Southampton later the same day. Sold in summer 2013, she loaded second-hand vehicles in Ipswich and departed for Famagusta on 14 June. She was renamed *Jaohar Discovery* and had become *Karazi* by the end of 2013. She was later converted to a livestock carrier trading mainly between Romania and Syria.

There are two container feeder ships named **Vanquish** and it seems almost unbelievable that both were used at the same time by a company named Cronus Logistics for a service linking Avonmouth to Warrenpoint. Although both are similar in length, this **Vanquish** (NLD, 2997gt/95) is smaller in terms of tonnage. An interesting ship, she was built at the J J Sietas shipyard on the outskirts of Hamburg and was the second of three sisterships designated as Type 157 by the builder. All three were built

for German owners for charter to Team Lines, a container feeder company linking Hamburg and Bremerhaven to Baltic ports. She was launched as **Wilhelm** on 20 May 1995 and underwent trials on 22 June. She was delivered as **Varmland** two days later. A decade later she was bought by Dutch owners and renamed **Vanquish**. She is seen at the start of a voyage to Warrenpoint on 10 February 2016.

After the two vessels named **Vanquish** were taken off the Cronus service, it has been left to a single ship to handle the cargoes. One of these was the **Emstal** (ATG, 3791gt/94). She was launched at Viana do Castelo in Portugal on 26 November 1994 and delivered on 30 December. Almost immediately she was taken on charter by Oldenburg-Portugiesische Dampfschiffs-Rhederi Kusen (OPDR), one of the oldest liner companies in Germany and arrived at Leixoes to load for her maiden voyage on 14 January 1995, henceforth linking this port and Lisbon to Europoort and Rotterdam. She was appropriately renamed **OPDR Douro** on 23 June 1995, reverting to **Emstal** at Bremerhaven on completion of the charter on 25 May 1999. She then traded in the Mediterranean linking Marsaxlokk, Naples Livorno and Genoa. On 11 June 2002 she was renamed **Portlink Runner** and returned to the Leixoes/Lisbon – Rotterdam route but with an additional call at Vigo. In March 2004 she reverted to **Emstal** and traded between Hamburg/Bremerhaven and Gdynia/Gdansk. She joined the Cronus service in mid-April 2016 and left in mid-June after being sold to Turkish owners and renamed **Ziad Junior**. The entrance to the lido is on the right of this photograph of the **Emstal** outward bound to Warrenpoint on 28 April 2016.

Our front cover depicted a vessel from the fleet of Faversham Ships, a comparatively young and successful British operator of small dry cargo ships. The **Verity** (IOM, 2601gt/01), one of ten ships currently in the company's fleet, was launched on 20 April 2001 at the Kootstertille shipyard of Tille Scheepsbouw as **Estime** and was delivered to Harlingen-based JR Shipping on 9 June. She joined the Union Transport fleet, now sadly defunct, as **Union Mercury** in 2004 and was acquired by Faversham Ships in 2008. We see her inward bound to Avonmouth with fertiliser from Amsterdam on 10 August 2012. After discharge she loaded rapeseed for Rotterdam.

Having discharged grain from Liepaja, the **Derk** (NLD, 2056gt/00) was outward bound from Avonmouth on 12 May 2009. Without further orders, she anchored in Blue Anchor Roads for several days until directed to sail for Eemshaven. Like many coastal vessels of her generation, she was built at two different shipyards. The construction of her hull was subcontracted to Ceskoslovenska Plavba Labska AS (CSPL) at Decin in the Czech Republic,

being launched on 17 September 1999. This hull was then towed to the Peters shipyard in Kampen, arriving on 18 October. There it was fitted out and completed as **Jan van Gent** on 8 January 2000. Owned in Delfzijl, the ship was managed by Wagenborg, a huge transport company in the north of the Netherlands. She remained in Wagenborg management following a sale to another Delfzijl owner in December 2005 when she was renamed **Derk**.

The **Vita** (ATG, 2497gt/90) was inward bound from the River Neath on 16 February 2012 and she loaded woodchips for Södertälje in Sweden. She was launched as **Emja** at the Bijlsma shipyard in Wartena on 16 November 1990 and was one of four ships ordered by German owner Klaus Braack, of Drochtersen. The design came from the Ferus Smit shipyard at Westerbroek and the order for construction was passed to the Bijlsma yard by Ferus Smit. The village of Wartena is on the Princess Margriet Canal and the delivery of the **Emja** from the shipyard was to prove challenging. The ship was 13 metres wide but the movable sections of bridges on the canal are only 12 metres wide. The solution was to put extra ballast in the hold and fill the double bottom tanks and then to navigate the ship beneath the fixed bridge sections. Once the ship arrived in Lemmer, the superstructure was added. The **Emja** was completed in late December 1990 and almost immediately was transferred to the ownership of a Dutch company. In 2004, she was acquired by Latvian owners and renamed **Vita**.

The **Bonay** (LVA, 1189gt/91) was inward bound with a cargo of forest products on 6 November 2016. She departed to Rotterdam four days later. She was launched at Harlingen on 9 October 1991 and delivered to Dutch owners as **Willy II** on 27 November. She was sold and renamed **Nordford** on 16 May 2001. A further sale within the Netherlands saw her name abbreviated to **Nord** when berthed at Europoort on 19 October 2004. She retained this name when sold to owners in Latvia in 2008 but eventually became **Bonay** in December 2011.

There are few urban or rural landscapes not now blighted by wind turbines. Although we do manufacture some parts for these in the UK, the vast majority are imported from overseas notably Portugal, Denmark, Germany and China. In recent years, specialised ships have been constructed for carrying the parts but it was the conventional *Kristin D* (BHS, 2035gt/97) that brought turbine tower sections from Leixoes on 7 October 2012. She was launched at the Tille shipyard in Kootstertille on 27 June 1997 and completed as *Heerestraat* on 11 September. She is an example of the Conofeeder 200 design and was the last of six examples built at the Tille yard. All were named after streets or bridges in Groningen and were owned by Armawa, a company established in the Netherlands in the mid-1990s. They were popular feeder ships and were chartered by companies such as Lys Line and Seawheel. The *Heerestraat* became *Jetstream* in 2004 and *Seawheel Express* in 2005. She was renamed *Kristin D* after sale to Norwegian owners in 2008.

Abis Shipping was established on 1 October 2007 and aimed to introduce innovative vessels for specific trades such as project and river/sea cargoes. The concept seemed to be successful until late autumn 2016 when twelve of the company's ships were subject to foreclosure by a bank. The **Abis Bremen** (NLD, 2978gt/11) was not one of the initial twelve. She is one of six sisterships in the B-series, all of which have their superstructure located at the forward part of the vessel. They were designed for the carriage of heavy cargoes and have proved extremely useful for carrying wind turbine sections. Her hull was built at the Partner Shipyard in Police, near Szczecin, with completion by Shipkit in Groningen. She is seen here when inward bound on 2 September 2013 with a cargo of coal from Amsterdam.

Outward bound on 28 August 2012, the **Alida** (ATG, 992gt/74) has a fascinating history. She was launched at the Barkmeier shipyard in Stroobos on 13 September 1974 and completed as **Arina Holwerda** on 1 November. She was the first of a group of eight ships of this standard design to be built at this shipyard in northern Holland, five of these being ordered by Hendrik and Piet Holwerda. Delivery was delayed because she was too large to pass the Blauwverlaat bridge over the Prinses Margrietkanaal on her way to Harlingen for trials and two large sections of the bridge had to be removed. Sales within the Netherlands saw her become **Spray** (1980),

Vissersbank (1986) and **Lida** (1990). In 2007, she carried a brewery from New Zealand to London. Some ex-pat Kiwis lamented the fact that they were unable to obtain any Speight's beer in London. In response, Speight's built and transported a fully operational brewery, the **Lida** leaving Dunedin on 25 July for a voyage lasting 76 days. In 2011 she was acquired by Mertech Marine, a South African company specialising in the recovery of submarine cables and was converted for this work. Once brought ashore, the components of the recovered cables are recycled, these being copper, steel, aluminium and polyethylene.

The **Wilson Garston** (BRB, 2270gt/89) was built at the Hugo Peters shipyard in Wewelsfleth on the River Stor, a tributary of the River Elbe in northern Germany. She was launched as **Pionier** on 2 September 1989 and completed during the following month. She was sold and renamed **Hanseatic Sea** in 2003 and was acquired by the Bergen-based Wilson Group in 2005.

Established by Paal Wilson in 1942, this company has grown into one of the largest shipping groups in northern Europe and in late 2016, it operated 112 ships with 80% owned and the others time-chartered. She was delivering a cargo of fertiliser when photographed on 16 February 2012.

In October 2012 the first steel was cut for a vessel named **Prelude** being built in South Korea. This will be the biggest floating vessel in the world and will be a floating liquefied natural gas platform. It will serve the Prelude and Concerto gas fields about 120 miles (200km) off the north-west coast of Australia. Equipment for the **Prelude** was manufactured all over the world and the gas metering equipment was manufactured in Gloucestershire. On 28 December 2013, the **Wilson Waal** (BRB, 1170gt/99) called at Sharpness to load some items for delivery the short distance to Avonmouth. We see her on the following day after discharging the equipment. She is heading for Blue Anchor Bay off the Somerset coast where she stayed for two days before heading to Rotterdam. The **Wilson Waal** was launched on 19 March 1999 at the yard of Československá plavba Labská, situated at Chvaletice on the River Elbe east of Prague in the Czech Republic. This yard has since become part of the Argo Group, a huge international logistics company. The ship is the sixth of seven known as the Elbe type and was delivered as **Podebrady** on 9 June 1999. She was renamed after joining the Wilson fleet in 2002.

The cargo brought to Avonmouth by **Wilson Waal** was taken to South Korea by the **Svenja** (ATG, 15026gt/10), a vessel too big for the dock at Sharpness. We see her approaching Avonmouth on 28 December 2013. She left in the early hours of 30 December, heading initially to Montoir in France to load further cargo. The yard of J J Sietas became well-known for the construction of coastal vessels but after remodelling the access to the yard it was able to build larger ships, the Type 183 **Svenja** being a good example. The ship is owned by SAL – Heavy Lift, a company whose first ship was also built at the Sietas yard. This was the sailing ship **Amoenitas** dating from 1865. The company remained in the ownership of the Heinrich family for almost 150 years until in 2011 the Japanese K-Line group acquired all shares. The **Svenja** is one of fifteen ships in the SAL fleet. She was launched on 25 September 2010 and delivered on 9 December. Each of her two cranes has a 1000 tonne lifting capacity and the ship is equipped with a dynamic positioning system.

Outward bound to Porto Marghera on 26 May 2013 was the heavy lift ship *Han Yi* (SGP, 10990gt/98), built at the Merwede shipyard at Hardinxveld. She was launched on 11 October 1997 and completed as *Sailer Jupiter* on 2 January 1998. She was the last of four sisterships and made her maiden voyage to Rijeka before sailing across to Buenos Aires and Santos. In August 1998 she was renamed *Enchanter* and in 2011 was acquired by owners in Singapore and renamed *Han Yi*. Her two cranes can each lift 400 tonnes. She had called to collect the cutter suction dredger *Evenlode* which had been delivered to the Port of Bristol in 1983 and had been sold to operators in Bangladesh.

This is one of sixteen vessels in the fleet of Hansa Heavy Lift (HHL) based in Hamburg. There are four different designs of ship within the fleet and the *HHL Venice* (ATG, 15549gt/10) is one of a pair designated as the P1 class. Each has a lifting capacity of 800 tonnes which can be achieved when No. 2 and No. 3 cranes work in tandem, each having a safe working load of 400 tonnes with an 18 metre outreach. The smaller No. 1 crane has a safe working load of 120 tonnes with a 16 metre outreach. We see the ship passing Battery Point on 20 July 2013 with the tug *Svitzer Anglia* on board. The *HHL Venice* had collected the tug from Tees Dock, Middlesbrough. In Avonmouth she loaded the tugs *HT Cutlass* and *HT Scimitar*, departing for Puerto Cabello in Venezuela with all three tugs on 25 July.

The **Refioglu** (TUR, 5997gt/97) was launched at the Shin Kurushima shipyard in Akitsu, near Hiroshima, on 17 December 1996 and completed as **Bay Sisters** on 24 March 1997. In March 2003 her name was changed to **Bay Sister** and she became **Sir Jacob** on 2 March 2004 when she began to trade mainly in South and Central America. By the time that she was sold and renamed **Refioglu** in early 2008, she was trading more widely. We see her inward bound from St Malo to Royal Portbury Dock on 12 November 2013 and she departed for Lisbon two days later with a cargo of grain. Sold within Turkey in 2015, she was renamed **Diamond Canakkale**. She is equipped with two 2-tonne cranes and one 25-tonne derrick.

Over the last two decades, the coastal shipping scene in northern Europe has come to be dominated by two companies. One of these is the Wilson Group in Norway and the other is Arklow Shipping in the Republic of Ireland. The latter has also invested in bigger tonnage and in 2003 took delivery of the *Arklow Wind* (IRL, 8938gt/03) built at Shimoneseki in Japan by Kyokuyo Zosen. The company took up an option for a second vessel and she was launched as *Arklow Willow* on 30 July 2004 with completion coming on 16 November. On 2 April 2016 she had the misfortune to collide with a fishing vessel off the coast of Greece, the latter being not properly lit and unable to change course as she was trawling. Later in 2016 the *Arklow Willow* was sold to McKeil Marine, a Canadian company celebrating its 60th anniversary in that year. The ship was taken over in Marseilles and delivered to Canada in order to be fitted out for her new work which would see her trading mainly on the Great Lakes carrying cement and other bulk cargoes. She was transferred to the Canadian flag and renamed *Florence Spirit* after Florence McKiel, wife of Evans McKeil who founded the company. We see the *Arklow Willow* nearing the end of a voyage from Dunkirk to Avonmouth on 19 July 2011; she left four days later for Jorf Lasfar in Morocco with a cargo of scrap.

The import of refrigerated food to Avonmouth was hugely important for much of the twentieth century. The last two decades, however, have seen such imports almost disappear and the arrival from Nelson (New Zealand) of the **Buzzard Bay** (LBR, 10381gt/92) on 16 April 2013 was unusual. She is a typical Japanese-built refrigerated vessel of the early 1990s. She was launched as **Royal Star** at the Shikoku shipyard in Takamatsu on 22 November 1991 and completed as **Chiquita Honshu** on 31 March 1992. She left Yokohama on her maiden voyage to New Zealand on the next day.

In early January 1995 she was chartered by Blue Star Line and reverted to her original name of **Royal Star**. On 5 December 1999 she was renamed **French Bay** having been sold to P&O Nedlloyd in the previous year. She became **Buzzard Bay** in July 2004 when bought by a Dutch company for management by Seatrade Groningen. Seatrade was established by five captain-owners of coastal vessels and in the 1960s began to specialise in refrigerated ships. In December 2013 the **Buzzard Bay** was sold to Russian owners and renamed **Baltic Pilgrim**.

The **Okiana** (IOM, 36324gt/04) was built by Oshima Shipbuilding and was launched on 8 December 2003. She was completed on 1 April 2004 and is one of four ships in the O-class. We see her arriving on 11 May 2015 with forest products from China; she sailed three days later to Tilbury, Terneuzen then on to Orkanger. H Westfal-Larsen established his own shipping company in Bergen in 1905, the year that Norway gained independence. The company suffered heavy losses in both world wars but has always sought niche markets, be they in the tanker, liner or, more recently, bulk trades. Her two gantry cranes each have a lifting capacity of 68 tonnes. Of special interest in this view is the towing method used by the bow tug, **Svitzer Moira**. Called the "sitting duck" style of towage by local crews, the bow tug edges as close as possible to the large inbound ship so that a heaving line can be passed to the tug. The photograph of the **Svitzer Moira** on page 77 shows that she has a powerful winch fitted on her fore section to permit bow-to-bow towage.

The **Posidana** (SGP, 39258gt/08) was outward bound to Setubal when photographed on 15 February 2016. She had arrived from Bremerhaven via Tilbury with a cargo of forest products that had originated in the Chinese port of Xingong. Built at the Oshima shipyard in Sakai, Japan, her keel was laid on 17 November 2005 but she was not launched until 22 August 2008 with completion on 24 October. The four ships in the P-class are the most modern in the fleet. The two gantry cranes, each with a 70-tonne lifting capacity, are a notable feature of the ship. Many of the Gearbulk ships which visited Royal Portbury Dock in the past also had such gantry cranes. Saga Welco, the legend on the ship's hull, is a joint pooling operation between Westfal-Larsen and Saga Forest Carriers which commenced operations on 1 October 2014. Both companies had been active in the break bulk / forest products sector since 1964 and 1991 respectively and the new pool offered shippers a total of 52 open-hatch vessels plus 2 newbuildings scheduled for delivery in 2017.

There is little to suggest from the photograph that the **Nordic Barents** (PAN, 27078gt/95) is a historically significant ship. In the late summer of 2010, she was selected to carry a cargo of 41,000 tonnes of iron ore concentrate from Kirkenes in northern Norway via the Northern Sea Route to China, passing through the Arctic and Russian waters. She was the first non-Russian ship permitted to make such a voyage which is a third shorter than the traditional route via the Mediterranean and Suez Canal. She is one of very few ships of her type with an Ice Class 1a classification which was demanded by the Russian authorities. Launched by Daewoo Heavy Industries at Okpo in South Korea on 9 January 1995, she was completed as **Federal Baffin** on 15 March. Later sales and changes of name saw her become **Baffin** (2005), **Ice Power II** and **Izara Princess** (2008) and **Cedar 4** and **Nordic Barents** (2009). We see her arriving from Swinoujscie in Poland with a cargo of forest products which had been loaded in China.

When she was photographed on 27 August 2013 the **Idship Bulker** (HKG, 17018gt/08) was heading for Avonmouth where she loaded scrap for delivery to Nemrut Bay in Turkey. She was launched at the Imabari Zosen shipyard in Marugame on 8 July 2008 and completed on 26 August. Working at eight different sites, this builder is Japan's biggest in terms of both tonnage and sales revenue. The **Idship Bulker** sailed on 2 September giving Gibraltar as her destination; again this would possibly have been for refuelling. Of special note are her funnel colours. The red funnel has a white J above a white band beneath which is a white L. These are the colours of well-known Danish owner J Lauritzen whose distinctive red-hulled ships used to be a common site in Bristol's City Docks. She carries the Lauritzen funnel colours as she is on time charter to them. She ran aground in the River Parana on 19 April 2005 when carrying a cargo of 26,099 tonnes of corn and soya meal from San Lorenzo, Argentina, to Rio de Janeiro. She was refloated five days later.

The **Sir Henry** (PHI, 11194/07) was launched at the Shikoku shipyard in Takamatsu, Japan, on 7 November 1996 and completed as **Rubin Lark** on 20 January 1997. She was bought by Turkish owners and renamed **Sebat** in 2015. We see her inward bound to Avonmouth on 26 April 2015 after making the short voyage across the Bristol Channel from Newport. She departed four days later with a cargo of scrap for Bordeaux and Barcelona.

The **Saint Fanouris** (CYP, 13697gt/07) was inward bound from Hull on 6 August 2016 to load scrap for Seville. She was launched at the Linahi Huipu shipyard in China on 20 February 2007 and delivered to Chinese owners as **Jing Shan 5** on 30 April. The shipyard opened in 2004 and this vessel, the first of two sisterships, was the eighth to be constructed. She seems never to have traded as **Jing Shan 5** but entered service as **Salvadora**. It seems astonishing that in August 2007, after only four months in service, she was detained after an inspection in Belfast with 23 deficiencies. Five of these led to her detention for five days and included inoperative radar, dirty engine room and inadequate general maintenance. She was sold and renamed **Bulk Valiant** in 2010 and became **Saint Fanouris** following another sale in 2014. The ship is named after Saint Fanourios, a martyr in the Greek Orthodox church. He has the honour of having a special cake dedicated to his honour, the fanouropita.

The **Spar Libra** (NIS, 32474gt/06) was outward bound to Setubal on 24 September 2015; she had delivered animal feed from Indonesia. She was built at the Chengxi shipyard at Jiangyin on the lower reaches of the Yangtze River. Launched on 26 January 2006, she was completed as **Bulk Navigator** on 26 April. By July she has been renamed **Arya Payk** and reverted to her original name in 2009, becoming **Spar Libra** two years later. She was involved in an unfortunate incident in early April 2016. She was anchored south of Chittagong with a cargo of 51,000 tonnes of Russian wheat loaded in Novorossiysk. After inspection by the Food Directorate of Bangladesh, the cargo was deemed to be unfit for human consumption.

It is not too often that a ship changes owner and name in our local port but we now see one that did so. She arrived as **Emerald** (MHL, 33044gt/10) on 1 August 2016 to discharge a part cargo of animal feed from Port Klang and whilst in port she was renamed **Ileana N**. We see her at the start of a voyage to Jorf Lasfar under her new name on 7 August. She is another ship to have been built at the Jinling Shipyard in Nanjing where she was completed as **Kavo Emerald** for well-known Greek shipping company Gourdomichalis Maritime in April 2010. She became **Emerald** in 2012.

The **GL Qushan** (HKG, 52186gt/11) was launched at the yard of Tsuneishi Zhoushan in China on 9 August 2011 and was delivered on 20 October to owner Glocal Maritime Ltd, a company incorporated in Hong Kong on 25 June 2010. We see her inward bound with a cargo of coal from Puerto Drummond in Colombia on 19 September 2012. She is one of the largest bulk carriers to visit the port and she required the assistance of six tugs as she made a cautious approach to Royal Portbury Dock. In January 2014 it was announced that she was to be sold along with a sistership to Star Bulk Carriers Corp in a fairly complex transaction. Once the sale had been completed the following month, the ship was renamed **Star Vega** and was chartered back to Glocal Maritime for a period of between 30 and 34 months at a daily rate of $15,000. This was expected to raise about $15 million in charter revenue during the minimum contact period.

Unusually we are including a second image of the same vessel to show the difference between the appearance of a large bulk carrier when almost fully laden and by contrast when in ballast. The **GL Qushan** is seen outward bound back to Portland for refuelling and then back to Puerto Drummond on 10 August 2012. This is a private port on the Caribbean Sea and is used to export coal brought by train from two open-cast mines operated by the Drummond family, the second largest producer of coal in Colombia. This family began mining coal in Alabama in 1935 and still owns a large mine there. It acquired the rights to mine coal in northern Colombia in the late

1980s and development started during the next decade. The traditional method of loading ships was to transfer the coal initially to barges which were then taken out to a waiting bulk carrier with loading by a floating crane. The Colombian government had been unhappy with this method since 2010, especially when a Drummond barge sank in 2013. It had insisted that all ships should be loaded directly by conveyor. Drummond failed to meet the deadline date of 1 January 2014 for the change and exports were banned until the conveyor system was completed in Spring 2014.

Twenty years ago, it would have been unusual for any tide to pass without a call by a small coastal tanker delivering refined oil products. The days of such small tankers have now passed and the oil products are brought less frequently by larger tankers such as **Bro Designer** (DIS, 11344gt/06). The last of four sisterships, she was launched at the Jinling shipyard in Nanjing, China, on 5 October 2005 and completed on 26 June 2006. Broström Tankers, a Swedish company, can date its history back to 1865. In January 2009 it was taken over by Maersk Tankers and thus became part of the Maersk Group. It would be fair to say that the takeover was not universally welcomed, especially when Maersk sought to transfer staff from Sweden to Denmark. The consequence was a partial demerger with some smaller vessels reverting to Swedish ownership by Thun Tankers. Tankers such as **Bro Designer** serve ports Cardiff, Belfast, Dublin and Plymouth in addition to Avonmouth and usually carry a combination of diesel, motor spirit and kerosene. We see her inward bound from Milford Haven on 11 February 2016.

The tanker **Terry** (MLT, 10321gt/99) was launched as **Pochary** at the Aker shipyard in Wismar on 22 July 1999 and completed on 29 October. The shipyard was established after the Second World War and for many years was known as the Mathias-Thesen-Werft. It passed through the hands of several owners especially after the collapse of the German Democratic Republic (East Germany) in 1990. In March 2016 the yard was bought by Genting Hong Kong, a Malaysian/Chinese shipping company. The tanker entered service for Lukoil under the Russian flag as **Murmansk**, her icebreaker bow intended to permit trade to northern ports during the winter months. She was sold and renamed **Murovdag** in 2006, becoming **Skledros** in 2012 and **Terry** after purchase by Greek owners in 2014. We see her inward bound with petroleum products from Rotterdam on 29 April 2016.

We now look at four tankers that have imported aviation fuel to Royal Portbury Dock. Many cargoes of aviation fuel are brought from Kuwait and the **Al Salam II** (KUW, 42798gt/07) was arriving from this port when seen on 15 February 2016. She was assisted by five tugs. The first of two sisterships, she was launched at the Daewoo shipyard in Okpo, South Korea, on the sunny morning of 3 October 2006 and delivered to the Kuwait Oil Tanker Company (KOTC) on 10 January 2007. This company had been established in April 1957 by a group of Kuwaiti investors who realised the importance of developing the country's oil industry and the need for sea transportation of oil and petroleum products. The Kuwaiti government acquired a 49% share in 1976 and took full control three years later.

The **Torgovy Bridge** (LBR, 27725gt/05) was starting a voyage to Bilbao on 28 July 2012 after delivering a cargo of aviation fuel. She was launched at the Admiralty Shipyard in St Petersburg on 29 April 2005 and completed on 2 September. She is owned by SCF Management Services Ltd, the initials SCF standing for Sovcomflot which is a Russian shipping company whose origins date back to the nineteenth century. It now specialises in the transport of oil and chemicals and 112 of its 140 ships are tankers.

The **Torgovy Bridge** is the fourth of eight sisterships able to carry five different oil products in ten tanks. All were built at the same shipyard from 2003 onwards. The bridge after which the ship was named is in Saint Petersburg. It crosses the Kryukov Canal and dates from 1785. The first bridge was a wooden one but it was extensively rebuilt in metal in 1960.

On 24 June 2016, the **UACC Ibn Al Haitham** (MLT, 42010gt/09) arrives from Kuwait with 65,000 tonnes of jet A1 fuel. Built by the New Times Shipbuilding Company at Jingjiang in China, she was delivered on 11 January 2009 to the Arabian Chemical Carriers Company, a fully controlled subsidiary of United Arab Chemical Carriers (UACC), and was the second of four sister vessels. This vessel illustrates perfectly the complexities of modern ship owning and operation. We have already referred to two owning companies but in fact she is registered in the ownership of Haitham Tankers Inc, a single-ship company. She is managed by Fleet Ship Management, based in Hong Kong, and is in a commercial pool of vessels operated by Straits Tankers, based in Singapore. She would then be chartered by an oil company, oil trader or shipping company for the carriage of petroleum products in her twelve tanks. For her first year in service, she was time chartered by DS Norden, a Danish shipping company. On this voyage, she had been chartered by the Kuwait Petroleum Corporation and the receiver of the cargo was Q8 Aviation, established in 1983 as part of the international division of the Kuwait Petroleum Corporation.

The **Abbey Road** (LBR, 42411gt/13) was a relatively new ship when she arrived from Sitra on 27 August 2013. Sitra is an island in Bahrain and the port handles the country's entire oil exports in addition to oil exports from north-eastern Saudi Arabia. The tanker, whose cargo of aviation fuel was destined for military storage, had been completed at the STX shipyard in Jinhae, South Korea. Although listed as a crude oil tanker, she is identified as one of nine product tankers by her managers, Zodiac Maritime, and is one of three sisterships, the others being named **Fulham Road** and **Kings Road.** Zodiac Maritime is based in Portman Street, in the West End of London, and manages over 150 vessels of various types and sizes. She departed for Falmouth two days later and after a stay of two weeks in Falmouth Bay she headed off to Ventspils in Latvia.

Another important liquid cargo to be imported to Royal Portbury Dock is molasses, a viscous substance totally different from highly refined aviation fuel. The **Maersk Etienne** (DIS, 26659gt/04) was photographed on 12 September 2013 as she was arriving with a cargo of molasses from San Jose, Guatemala. She was launched on 13 October 2003 at the Jinling shipyard in Nanjing, China, and completed as **Bro Etienne** for Swedish tanker owner Broström on 10 November 2004. In January 2009 the Broström company was taken over by the Maersk group and the ship was renamed **Maersk Etienne**. On 18 January 2015 she was involved in a collision with the bulk carrier **Coral Opal** in the Irbenskiy Strait near Mikelbaka lighthouse off the coast of Latvia when on passage to Riga from Rouen. There were no casualties or injuries in the incident.

The **Oradana** (DIS, 1639gt/71) was inward bound to No. 3 Oil Berth at Avonmouth on 18 March 2013. At this berth she was the second of two coastal tankers to load a cargo of molasses from the **Chembulk Lindy Alice** which had arrived on the previous day. The **Oradana** departed for Silloth on the next tide. She has an interesting history, having been launched at the Clemna shipyard in La Spezia on 7 August 1971 and completed as **Scarlino Primo** for Italian owners on 13 October. In May 1989 she was sold to M H Simonsen, a Danish tanker owning company. She arrived at the shipyard in Svendborg on 11 August 1989 to be upgraded to Danish standards and to be converted for the carriage of vegetable oils. She was notable in being the first double-hulled tanker in the Simonsen fleet and was thus able to carry refined edible oils. Her main trade, however, was intended to be the export of molasses from Poland and her first cargo after conversion was one of molasses loaded at Gdansk on 1 November 1989. Later in 2013 she was sold to owners in Angola and was renamed **Santo Muhongo III**. Since then she has been based in Luanda.

Before we move on to a selection of work boats and harbour craft, we include an image from an area almost totally neglected by ship photographers. This is the eastern end of the grassy area that leads down to the navigation marker and is close to a wooded area with footpaths. The *Conmar Elbe* passes Battery Point on 31 May 2016 at the end of a voyage from Liverpool. At the time she was trading between Liverpool, Bilbao and Royal Portbury Dock. She was constructed at the Hugo Peters shipyard at Wewelsfleth, a small town on the western bank of the River Stör which flows into the Elbe north of Hamburg. Shipbuilding at the location can be dated back to 1757 and the Peters shipyard opened in 1871. Like many other shipyards in Germany, this one now survives by constructing mega yachts. This ship was launched on 6 October 2001 and completed as *Euro Storm* on 28 December. She became *Conmar Elbe* in 2012 and it is worth noting that she returned to Wewelsfleth for overhaul in January 2017.

Over the last two decades, many ports have contracted out survey and dredging services and one of the most frequently used companies to benefit from this is UK Dredging, a subsidiary of Associated British Ports, which has a fleet of one grab dredger and three suction dredgers in addition to two general purpose vessels. As many readers will know, siltation is a constant problem in the Bristol Channel and a UK Dredging vessel assists regularly in maintaining an adequate depth of water in the navigation channel. The work is carried out over a low water period. On 28 April 2014, the **UKD Bluefin** (GBR, 4171gt/97) was working. She was built by Ferguson Shipbuilders at Port Glasgow and was launched into the River Clyde on 22 January 1997 and completed on 30 April. She is a trailing suction hopper dredger with suction pipes on both port and starboard sides. The dredged material can be pumped ashore or discharged through bottom doors.

The **Sand Heron** (GBR, 3751gt/90) was the first of two sisterships built at the Merwede shipyard in Hardinxveld. She was launched on 10 March 1990 and completed on 4 May. We see her heading towards Avonmouth on 1 June 2013. She usually visits the Bristol Channel when our usual dredger Welsh Piper is not available but on this occasion her visit was remarkably brief. She was arriving from Southampton via Plymouth and she returned to the Solent three days later. On 30 July 2001, she was involved in a collision in the English Channel with a French fishing boat which had failed to give way in accordance with Collision Regulations. There were no casualties and only slight damage to the dredger. In November 2015, Georgina Carlo-Paat became master of the **Sand Heron**, the first female master of a vessel in the UK marine aggregate dredging sector.

The lightvessel **Planet** is indeed a historic vessel. She was built by Philip & Sons at Dartmouth for the Mersey Docks and Harbour Board. Launched on 24 May 1960, she passed into the ownership of Trinity House in September 1972. She had become the final manned lightvessel on the Mersey and by 1989 when she was demanned she had become the last manned vessel of her kind in the UK. Sold in 1992, she was brought to the Mersey and was initially berthed in Birkenhead but moved to Albert Dock in Liverpool in 2006 since when she was used as a cafe/bar and museum. However, in 2016 she was controversially taken over by the Canal and River Trust which was owed about £10,000 in unpaid mooring fees. She was towed to Sharpness and offered for sale with a £100,000 price tag. We see her passing Battery Point on passage to Sharpness on 24 September 2016, towed by **MTS Indus**. The tug is off the image to the right as we have chosen to concentrate on the **Planet**.

As soon as the construction of Hinkley-C power station was given final approval, various vessels arrived at Avonmouth to prepare for the major civil engineering works. We look at three of them in this book. Built in 2012, the **Wavewalker 1** is an innovative eight-legged "walking" jack-up barge, especially made to operate in rough seas, surf zones, beaches and other intertidal locations. Its bi-directional movement allows it to move and relocate without floating and it can reach overall bi-directional walking speeds of up to 40 metres per hour. The design, construction and operation of this platform were a joint effort of Fugro Seacore and Van Oord/Wicks. Together they established the 50/50 joint venture company WaveWalker BV, which is registered in the Netherlands. It was built at the Neptune Shipyard in Hardinxveld-Giessendam in the Netherlands. We see the barge heading towards Royal Portbury Dock towed from Falmouth by **MTS Viscount** which is out of the picture. After being prepared for work, the rig was towed to the Hinkley Point construction site on 26 November 2016.

As construction of Hinkley C power station progresses, there will be an increasing number of vessels involved for a wide variety of tasks. The **MCS Ailsa** (GBR, 479gt/96), classed as a deck cargo vessel but generally referred to as a multicat, was built at the Sliedrecht shipyard of A Baars Azn which has specialised in the construction of workboats and dredgers since 1888. Originally named **Katliz**, she was acquired by Maritime Craft Services and renamed in 2003. In 2011 she was substantially refurbished and upgraded; the work included the fitting of two new Caterpillar engines. Five additional twin cabins were fitted which makes her even more popular as a diving support vessel.

The **Dutch Pearl** (NLD, 254gt/10) was built at the Bomex 4M shipyard on the Bega River in Zrenjanin, Serbia. Delivered in April 2010 to Landfall Marine Contractors, she is an ideal multipurpose vessel. With a shallow draught, she can work in a wide range of marine situations and is fitted for pushing in addition to conventional towing astern. She has a bollard pull of 46.2 tonnes. This photograph, along with that on the previous page, was taken on 29 November 2016.

Having seen the **Dutch Pearl**, we now take a closer look at some tugs. The **Pantodynamos** (PAN, 859gt/71) is no ordinary tug. Launched at the Schichau shipyard in Bremerhaven on 27 November 1970, she was completed as **Seetrans I** for Hamburg-based owners in April 1971. She remained in German ownership following a sale in 1975 which saw her renamed **Raga I** and again in 1979 when she was became **Hanseatic**

for Petersen & Alpers. The next sale in 1987 saw her remain in Hamburg ownership when she joined the Fairplay fleet as **Fairplay XIV**. She remained with that company until acquired by Greek owners and renamed **Pantodynamos** in 2007. She called at Avonmouth to collect local Svitzer tug **Warrior III** which had been sold to owners in Piraeus and had been renamed **Christos XXV**.

It is occasionally necessary to charter tugs when local fleet members are unavailable through drydocking or temporary transfer to another area. Sometimes the opportunity is taken to test a specific vessel or design in order to assess its suitability for work in the Bristol Channel. In the winter of 2013/2014, the *Triton* (NLD, 476gt/08) was chartered from Iskes Towage and Salvage, a company based in the Dutch port of Ijmuiden. She was launched as *Pinar* at the Dearsan Gemi shipyard in Tuzla, near Istanbul, on 5 January 2008 and completed as *Triton* on 23 May. On 8 January 2014 she was one of five tugs assisting the bulk carrier *City of Dubrovnik* inward bound with a cargo of coal.

The **Thorngarth** (GBR, 365gt/82) passes Battery Point on 9 April 2014. Although Cory Towage had won a 5-year contract in 1991 to supply tugs to assist tankers visiting the oil terminals in Milford Haven, the towage company was finding it difficult to meet the requirements of the oil companies requiring the tugs. Its search for suitable secondhand tugs took Cory to Japan and it bought the **Tenzan**. This tug had been launched by Hanasaki Zosensho at Yokosuka on 8 August 1983 and completed on 6 September. She was bought by Cory in July 1991 but was not handed over until December. She left Yokohama for the long voyage to the UK on 8 January 1992. Following drydocking, she began work at Milford Haven in April 1992. After leaving Milford Haven, she worked on the River Mersey and arrived at Avonmouth in Autunn 2010. Sold to Romanian owners in late August 2016 and renamed **BSV Norvegia**, she left Avonmouth for Constanta on 1 September.

During 2016, our home-based tug fleet was reduced to only three vessels. One of these was **Portgarth** which we have seen in a previous edition. She was joined by sisterships **Svitzer Ellerby** and **Svitzer Moira** which came from the Humber. Both built by Imamura at Kure in Japan, the **Svitzer Moira** (GBR, 267gt/98) was launched on 19 November 1997 and completed on 9 January 1998 as **Peng Chau** for the Hong Kong Salvage and Towage Co Ltd. In September 1999 she was purchased by Howard Smith Towage and renamed **Peng** for the delivery voyage to the Humber where she became **Lady Moira**. In 2001, Howard Smith Towage was taken over by Adsteam but this tug did not change her name until 2007 when she became **Svitzer Moira** after Svitzer had taken over Adsteam. She arrived in the Bristol Channel from the Humber on 26 June 2011. We see her on 15 May 2012, clearly a day of bright sunlight and heavy showers.

The hull of **Svitzer Melton** (GBR, 381gt/96) was built by Stocznia Polnonca (Northern Shipyard) in Gdansk and the tug was completed at the Damen shipyard in Gorinchem. Delivered for work at Felixstowe as **Melton** in May 1996, she was part of a large tug order for Howard Smith which had taken over Alexandra Towing in 1993. Adsteam took over Howard Smith in May 2001 but this tug was not renamed at the time and she became **Svitzer Melton** in 2007 after Adsteam had itself been taken over by Svitzer. She left Felixstowe for delivery to Swansea on 6 November 2012. In this image, she is assisting with the docking of the tanker **Al Salam II** on 15 February 2016.

There have often been occasions when it has been necessary to call on additional tugs to work at our local port. With Svitzer having lost the contract to serve ports in South Wales, the extra tugs have to be summoned from Swansea or Milford Haven. The **Svitzer Gelliswick** (GBR, 490gt/08) is one of nine new tugs built to handle the tankers delivering liquefied natural gas to the two new terminals that opened in Milford Haven in 2009. The tugs to be used at the South Hook terminal were given red-topped funnels to set them apart for this work but they are sometimes released for other duties.

The **Svitzer Gelliswick** was heading back to her home port on 6 August 2016 after assisting with the docking of a tanker at Royal Portbury Dock on the previous tide. She is one of three tugs designed by Svitzer and built at the Qingdao Qianin shipyard in China, being launched on 19 February 2008 and delivered during April. On entry into service, all three tugs failed to live up to expectations and were sent to Vigo for "repair and modification", the long delivery voyage from China being blamed for poor workmanship during construction.

Making a very rare visit to the Bristol Channel, the **Leo Spirit** (PAN, 60825gt/12) passes Battery Point on 7 November 2016. She was launched at the Shin Kurushima shipyard in Toyohashi on 28 November 2011 and was completed on 12 June 2012.